Dr S
Sec

Coordinator on leave

0117
2428808

_____

_____

RECIPE
From the kitchen of

Ingredients

Directions

Notes

RECIPE

From the kitchen of _____

Ingredients

Directions

Notes

RECIPE

From the kitchen of

Ingredients

Directions

Notes

RECIPE
From the kitchen of _____

Ingredients

Directions

Notes

RECIPE
From the kitchen of _____

Ingredients

Directions

Notes

RECIPE
From the kitchen of

Ingredients

Directions

Notes

RECIPE

From the kitchen of _____

Ingredients

Directions

Notes

RECIPE
From the kitchen of _____

Ingredients

Directions

Notes

RECIPE
From the kitchen of _____

Ingredients

Directions

Notes

RECIPE
From the kitchen of _____

Ingredients

_____   _____
_____   _____
_____   _____
_____   _____
_____

Directions

_____
_____
_____
_____
_____
_____
_____
_____
_____
_____

Notes

_____
_____
_____
_____
_____

RECIPE
From the kitchen of _____

Ingredients

Directions

Notes

RECIPE
From the kitchen of _____

Ingredients

Directions

Notes

RECIPE

From the kitchen of

Ingredients

Directions

Notes

RECIPE
From the kitchen of _____

Ingredients

Directions

Notes

RECIPE

From the kitchen of _____

Ingredients

Directions

Notes

RECIPE
From the kitchen of _____

Ingredients

_____   _____
_____   _____
_____   _____
_____   _____
_____   _____

Directions

_____
_____
_____
_____
_____
_____
_____
_____
_____
_____

Notes

_____
_____
_____
_____
_____
_____

RECIPE
From the kitchen of

Ingredients

Directions

Notes

RECIPE
From the kitchen of _____

Ingredients

Directions

Notes

RECIPE
From the kitchen of

Ingredients

Directions

Notes

RECIPE
From the kitchen of _____

Ingredients

Directions

Notes

RECIPE

From the kitchen of

Ingredients

Directions

Notes

RECIPE
From the kitchen of _____

Ingredients

Directions

Notes

RECIPE
From the kitchen of _____

Ingredients

Directions

Notes

RECIPE

From the kitchen of _____

Ingredients

Directions

Notes

RECIPE
From the kitchen of _____

Ingredients

Directions

Notes

RECIPE

From the kitchen of _____

Ingredients

Directions

Notes

RECIPE
From the kitchen of

Ingredients

Directions

Notes

RECIPE
From the kitchen of

Ingredients

Directions

Notes

RECIPE
From the kitchen of _____

Ingredients

Directions

Notes

RECIPE   _____
From the kitchen of _____

Ingredients

_____ _____
_____ _____
_____ _____
_____ _____
_____ _____

Directions

_____
_____
_____
_____
_____
_____
_____
_____
_____
_____

Notes

_____
_____
_____
_____
_____

RECIPE
From the kitchen of

Ingredients

Directions

Notes

RECIPE
From the kitchen of _____

Ingredients

Directions

Notes

RECIPE
From the kitchen of

Ingredients

Directions

Notes

RECIPE
From the kitchen of _____

Ingredients

Directions

Notes

RECIPE

From the kitchen of _____

Ingredients

Directions

Notes

RECIPE

From the kitchen of _____

Ingredients

Directions

Notes

RECIPE
From the kitchen of _____

Ingredients

_____ _____
_____ _____
_____ _____
_____ _____
_____

Directions

_____
_____
_____
_____
_____
_____
_____
_____
_____
_____

Notes

_____
_____
_____
_____
_____
_____

RECIPE
From the kitchen of _____

Ingredients

Directions

Notes

RECIPE
From the kitchen of _____

Ingredients

Directions

Notes

RECIPE
From the kitchen of _____

Ingredients

Directions

Notes

RECIPE
From the kitchen of

Ingredients

Directions

Notes

RECIPE

From the kitchen of _____

Ingredients

Directions

Notes

RECIPE
From the kitchen of _____

Ingredients

Directions

Notes

RECIPE
From the kitchen of _____

Ingredients

Directions

Notes

RECIPE

From the kitchen of _____

Ingredients

Directions

Notes

RECIPE
From the kitchen of _____

Ingredients

Directions

Notes

RECIPE
From the kitchen of _____

Ingredients

Directions

Notes

RECIPE
From the kitchen of _____

Ingredients

Directions

Notes

RECIPE
From the kitchen of

Ingredients

Directions

Notes

RECIPE
From the kitchen of

Ingredients

Directions

Notes

RECIPE
From the kitchen of _____

Ingredients

Directions

Notes

RECIPE
From the kitchen of _____

Ingredients

Directions

Notes

RECIPE
From the kitchen of

Ingredients

Directions

Notes

RECIPE
From the kitchen of _____

Ingredients

Directions

Notes

RECIPE
From the kitchen of

Ingredients

Directions

Notes

RECIPE
From the kitchen of _____

Ingredients

Directions

Notes

RECIPE

From the kitchen of _____

Ingredients

Directions

Notes

RECIPE
From the kitchen of _____

Ingredients

Directions

Notes

RECIPE
From the kitchen of _____

Ingredients

Directions

Notes

RECIPE

From the kitchen of _____

Ingredients

Directions

Notes

RECIPE

From the kitchen of _____

Ingredients

Directions

Notes

RECIPE
From the kitchen of _____

Ingredients

Directions

Notes

RECIPE
From the kitchen of _____

Ingredients

Directions

Notes

RECIPE
From the kitchen of _____

Ingredients

Directions

Notes

RECIPE
From the kitchen of

Ingredients

Directions

Notes

RECIPE

From the kitchen of _____

Ingredients

_____   _____
_____   _____
_____   _____
_____   _____
_____   _____

Directions

_____
_____
_____
_____
_____
_____
_____
_____
_____
_____

Notes

_____
_____
_____
_____
_____

RECIPE
From the kitchen of

Ingredients

Directions

Notes

RECIPE
From the kitchen of _____

Ingredients

Directions

Notes

RECIPE
From the kitchen of _____

Ingredients

Directions

Notes

RECIPE
From the kitchen of _____

Ingredients

Directions

Notes

RECIPE
From the kitchen of _____

Ingredients

Directions

Notes

RECIPE

From the kitchen of _____

Ingredients

Directions

Notes

RECIPE
From the kitchen of

Ingredients

Directions

Notes

RECIPE
From the kitchen of _____

Ingredients

Directions

Notes

RECIPE

From the kitchen of _____

Ingredients

Directions

Notes

RECIPE
From the kitchen of

Ingredients

Directions

Notes

RECIPE

From the kitchen of _____

Ingredients

Directions

Notes

RECIPE
From the kitchen of _____

Ingredients

Directions

Notes

RECIPE
From the kitchen of

Ingredients

Directions

Notes

RECIPE
From the kitchen of _____

Ingredients

Directions

Notes

RECIPE

From the kitchen of

Ingredients

Directions

Notes

RECIPE
From the kitchen of _____

Ingredients

_____ _____
_____ _____
_____ _____
_____ _____
_____ _____

Directions

_____
_____
_____
_____
_____
_____
_____
_____
_____
_____

Notes

_____
_____
_____
_____
_____

RECIPE

From the kitchen of _____

Ingredients

Directions

Notes

RECIPE

From the kitchen of _____

Ingredients

Directions

Notes

RECIPE
From the kitchen of

Ingredients

Directions

Notes

RECIPE
From the kitchen of _____

Ingredients

Directions

Notes

RECIPE
From the kitchen of _____

Ingredients

Directions

Notes

RECIPE
From the kitchen of _____

Ingredients

Directions

Notes

RECIPE
From the kitchen of _____

Ingredients

Directions

Notes

RECIPE

From the kitchen of _____

Ingredients

Directions

Notes

RECIPE
From the kitchen of _____

Ingredients

Directions

Notes

RECIPE
From the kitchen of _____

Ingredients

_____   _____
_____   _____
_____   _____
_____   _____
_____   _____

Directions

_____
_____
_____
_____
_____
_____
_____
_____
_____
_____

Notes

_____
_____
_____
_____
_____

RECIPE
From the kitchen of _____

Ingredients

Directions

Notes

RECIPE
From the kitchen of _____

Ingredients

Directions

Notes

RECIPE
From the kitchen of _____

Ingredients

Directions

Notes

RECIPE

From the kitchen of _____

Ingredients

_____ _____
_____ _____
_____ _____
_____ _____
_____ _____

Directions

_____
_____
_____
_____
_____
_____
_____
_____
_____
_____
_____

Notes

_____
_____
_____
_____
_____
_____

RECIPE

From the kitchen of

Ingredients

Directions

Notes

RECIPE

From the kitchen of _____

Ingredients

_____   _____
_____   _____
_____   _____
_____   _____
_____   _____

Directions

_____
_____
_____
_____
_____
_____
_____
_____
_____
_____

Notes

_____
_____
_____
_____
_____

RECIPE

From the kitchen of

Ingredients

Directions

Notes

RECIPE _____
From the kitchen of _____

Ingredients

_____   _____
_____   _____
_____   _____
_____   _____
_____   _____

Directions

_____
_____
_____
_____
_____
_____
_____
_____
_____
_____

Notes

_____
_____
_____
_____
_____

RECIPE
From the kitchen of _____

Ingredients

_____   _____
_____   _____
_____   _____
_____   _____
_____

Directions

_____
_____
_____
_____
_____
_____
_____
_____
_____
_____

Notes

_____
_____
_____
_____
_____